READERS FOR TEENS

Lost in the Woods

Luiz H. Rose

Maiza Fatureto

Tereza Sekiya

Series coordinator
Sérgio Varela

CAMBRIDGE
UNIVERSITY PRESS

University Printing House, Cambridge CB2 8BS, United Kingdom

One Liberty Plaza, 20th Floor, New York, NY 10006, USA

477 Williamstown Road, Port Melbourne, VIC 3207, Australia

314–321, 3rd Floor, Plot 3, Splendor Forum, Jasola District Centre, New Delhi – 110025, India

103 Penang Road, #05-06/07, Visioncrest Commercial, Singapore 238467

Cambridge University Press is part of the University of Cambridge.

It furthers the University's mission by disseminating knowledge in the pursuit of education, learning and research at the highest international levels of excellence.

http://cambridge.org/elt/readersforteens/

© Cambridge University Press 2007

This publication is in copyright. Subject to statutory exception and to the provisions of relevant collective licensing agreements, no reproduction of any part may take place without the written permission of Cambridge University Press.

First published 2007

20 19 18 17 16 15 14 13

Printed in Great Britain by CPI Group (UK) Ltd, Croydon CR0 4YY

A catalogue record for this publication is available from the British Library

ISBN 978-0-521-04315-1 paperback

Cambridge University Press has no responsibility for the persistence or accuracy of URLs for external or third-party internet websites referred to in this publication, and does not guarantee that any content on such websites is, or will remain, accurate or appropriate.

Illustrations by Rogério Soud

Art direction, book design and layout services: A+ Comunicação, Brazil

Contents

Chapter 1
The idea   5

Chapter 2
The plan   7

Chapter 3
Getting lost   11

Chapter 4
The lesson learned   20

Chapter 1
The idea

David, Pete, and Frank are very good friends. They study together at Wells International School. They are in seventh grade and they are 12. These three friends have a lot in common. They love sports, adventure, and danger. They like to do what they want and they don't listen to their parents very much. At the moment they are all grounded.

Pete is surfing the Internet. He sees the Camp Coby Web site, and talks with David and Frank via the Internet.

"Let's go to Camp Coby."

"Good idea, I love to go camping," says David.

"Yes, we can swim, go canoeing, ride horses, make a campfire and tell stories at night. It sounds so great!" says Frank.

"But there's a problem," Pete says. "We're grounded."

"Let's ask our parents," suggests David.

"OK," Pete and Frank agree.

The boys talk to their parents and ask for their permission to go camping on the weekend. The answers are all the same.

"Go camping? Forget it, David. You're grounded!" says David's father.

"No, you can't. You're staying home!" says Frank's mother.

"No way!" say Pete's parents.

Chapter 2
The plan

David, Pete, and Frank are very sad. They really want to go camping! It's very important to them, but their parents don't understand.

The next day at school, they meet again.

"It's not fair!" David says.

Pete agrees: "They can't tell us what to do! We have to go!"

"But what can we do?"

David says, "We can go and come back on the same day! We can get a bus to Camp Coby, spend the day there, and come back at the end of the day."

Frank replies, "But we don't have any money!"

"No problem, Frank," says Pete. "We simply sneak in and enjoy the place!"

"We can take water and food," suggests David.

"We don't need a lot of things. Forget about the tent, sleeping bags, and coats. We can be back before it gets dark."

"What about our parents?" asks Frank.

"We don't need to tell them!" says Pete.

"We just tell them we are going to the library on Saturday," says David.

"So this is the plan. We put everything in our backpacks and meet at the bus station at seven o'clock," says David. "We can get the bus there, and arrive at Camp Coby before 10 A.M."

On Saturday, the three friends meet at the bus station, and they take the bus to Camp Coby. They are all very happy and excited.

Chapter 3
Getting lost

Nobody sees David, Pete, and Frank. They get into Camp Coby without any problems. Now they can finally relax and enjoy the place. They go hiking. After some time, they decide to stop and rest for a few minutes.

Frank has an idea.

"Hey, let's climb that mountain!"

"Yes, that's a good idea. We can see the entire camp from there," says Pete.

They go off the main trail and start to climb the mountain.

At the top, they find an amazing view of the camp.

"That's the Camp's main lodge," says David.

"Yes, look at that beautiful lake!" says Frank.

"We can go canoeing," suggests Pete.

"Excellent idea!" the others say.

"Look, there are some people riding horses over there," says David.

"Yes, very nice! Let's go back down," says Frank.

The boys are very excited.

After canoeing for an hour, the boys decide to have lunch. They eat their sandwiches and drink some water.

After lunch, they go horseback riding. They meet other kids and make some new friends. The kids come from many different countries. They tell interesting stories about their towns and schools.

After that, their new friends decide to go canoeing, but Frank, Pete, and David want to do something else.

They start to walk away, but Pete notices something.

"Shhhhhh! Hey, there's something there," he says.

"What is it? Let's take a look!" David suggests.

"Look! It's a rabbit! It's running!" says David. "Come on, come on!"

The boys run after the little brown rabbit. They run into the woods. They're having fun trying to catch the rabbit. They run and run, but the rabbit is very fast.

Finally they stop running after the rabbit.

After a long day at Camp Coby, the boys are tired.

They see a big tree, and they sit under it. They fall asleep.

When they wake up it's almost dark. The boys are far from the camp's main lodge.

"Wow, it's late!" says David.

"Let's go back!" says Pete.

"OK, but where's the way out?" asks Frank.

"Gee, I don't know," says David.

"Let's try this way," Pete says.

"OK," Frank and David agree.

In the meantime, the boys' parents are getting worried. They try to call them, but the boys don't answer their cell phones. They go to the library, but the boys are not there. It's getting dark, and there's no news about the kids.

"Where are our boys?" asks Frank's mother.

"I don't know, but I suspect they are at the camp right now," says David's father.

"I agree with you," says Pete's father. "These kids always do what they want!"

All the parents decide to go to Camp Coby to see if the boys are there. They have to go before it gets really dark.

The boys keep walking, but they can't find the way back.

"This place is very big! Where's the camp's main lodge?" asks Frank.

"I don't know," David replies. "Let's keep walking!"

They continue to walk, but they can't find the way out. They're completely lost.

"Let's call our parents," suggests Pete. They reach for their cell phones, but they don't have them. Their cell phones are at home.

It's dark now, and it's getting cold. The three friends are not enjoying the camp anymore. In fact, they are getting really worried now.

The boys keep walking, but it's dark and they can't see very well. There is a big hole in the ground. David doesn't see it. He starts falling slowly into the hole, but he grabs some branches.

Chapter 4
The lesson learned

Suddenly, two big hands grab David and pull him back up. When he looks up, he sees his father.

The boys are happy now. David is safe. They can all go home. But the boys' parents are not very happy.

"Don't ever do this again!" says David's father, holding him tight. "You can get seriously hurt! And so can your friends!"

David's mother is angry, too.

David feels really bad.

The camp coordinator is there, too. He talks to the boys very seriously.

"You can't do whatever you want. You have to listen to your parents. A good relationship between parents and children comes from confidence and trust. A lie can destroy all that."

Now David, Pete, and Frank understand. They have a chance to start over. The lesson is learned!

A week later, the three boys are back at school. They want to play soccer in the afternoon, but they can't. They are grounded. This time, they stay home! They don't want to get in trouble again.